I0435946

Bleed Ink: A Self-Publishing Guide

Teresa Mummert

Published by Teresa Mummert, 2013.

BLEED INK: A SELF-PUBLISHING GUIDE

First edition. October 28, 2013.

Copyright © 2013 Teresa Mummert.

ISBN: 978-1530851485

Written by Teresa Mummert.

DREAM BIG

SO YOU WANT TO BE A writer? Awesome! Writing is a great stress reliever. We all have our reasons for wanting to put pen to paper or fingers to keyboard. I personally just love to tell stories. I've been called *Storybook Teresa* since as far back as I can remember. I love to talk and talk and talk and... well, you get the point.

Becoming a writer is more work than you could ever imagine. There is getting the story out, covers, editing, promoting and hopefully a little celebration. I am often asked how I went about putting a book out for sale. I don't have all of the answers, but I can tell you the process I went through and hopefully save you a headache or two.

The first thing you need to do is know what story you want to tell. Some authors live by outlining and plotting out their novels. I am what is known as a 'pantser'. I don't write outlines or even know how my story will end in most cases. It is more exciting for me to live the story through the characters and be as surprised as the reader how it all ends. Many authors plot out a general outline. There is no right or wrong way to write your manuscript. It just depends on what you are most comfortable with. I would suggest using a dry erase board to plot out your story line if you chose to do so. I also like to search online for images of people who resemble my character and save the pictures. I then make a 'character file' using Microsoft Word or paint shop, where I list all of the physical characteristics and backstories of the characters, along with the picture. If your novel has several main characters, it can be hard to remember eye color or family history for each one. This just makes things a little easier. I like to do my writing in Microsoft Word[1]. It is very user-friendly and the program most editors are familiar working with.

I also write out of order. This can become very confusing if you jump around a lot. I make sure to mark in a large font where I need to add to the story so I can go back later and fill in plot holes. If your story is told over a timeline, it may make things easier to label the chapters as dates to ensure you do not skip any important days. You can always go back later and change the titles. Track Changes is what most editors will use when making corrections in your manuscript, so I advise getting the hang of it as soon as possible.

An excellent way to plan out how much you need to write a day is to pick a release date. I generally choose a Tuesday because it gives you a full week of sales for the bestseller lists. Make sure your release date gives you plenty of time in case an issue arises. If you are a fast writer, you may only need three months to write your novel, but you will also need several weeks for editing and formatting. I would contact your editor to find out their turnaround time and to make sure they are available for when you need them. Editors tend to book months in advance so I would take care of this step as soon as possible. See my chapter on Editors for more information.

Once you have a release date and a general idea of how long you want your novel to be, divide the word count by the number

---

1. http://search.microsoft.com/en-us/DownloadResults.aspx?rf=sp&q=word

of days you have to complete your work. This will tell you how much writing you need to do each day to finish on time.

If a story isn't coming to you, it is okay to shelf that book and work on a different project. Being a writer isn't about getting from A to Z in X number of days. Sometimes we have to just follow our imagination and let it lead the way. Most of my book ideas come from dreams that I expand into a story. I use a lot of music to help me get into the right mood of the character. An excellent program for this is Spotify[2]. I use it to create custom playlists for each of my novels. The best thing about it? It has a free version! You can't go wrong with free! I will talk about how to use Spotify as a promotional tool later as well.

Generally, a novella is a book that consists of less than fifty thousand words. This can vary by genre. Some stories can be told in seventy thousand words while others may take one hundred thousand or a series of books to tell the whole tale. However you choose to write your story is up to you. This is a personal choice. Once you've bled onto the paper, that is when things can get confusing for new authors. This is what I am going to try to help you with.

---

2. https://www.spotify.com/us/signup-for-spotify/?utm_source=N763.doubleclick.co-mOX2335&utm_medium=paid_102610902%7C0&utm_cam-paign=7860735&utm_content=us500761

BETA READERS

———

BETA READERS ARE AN important step in the book writing process. They can be a friend, coworker or a professional editor. Their job is to basically read over your manuscript to let you know if they find any plot holes, or if the story flows.

It is essential to have a second or third set of eyes on your story because what you see in your head may not have translated precisely to paper. If you do not know someone who would be willing to beta read, post in a reading group online, such as Facebook. Readers are always looking for something new and a free book is hard to pass up.

You wouldn't want to put out a novel that has not been read. They can also give you advice on what they liked about the story and what they think needs improvement. It can be hard to hear negative feedback about something you worked so hard on, but better to hear it from one than thousands.

After you have taken advice from your beta readers and corrected any inconsistencies, it is time to move forward with editing.

EDITING

WHETHER YOU HAVE BEEN published with one of the Big 5 publishers (Penguin Random House, Macmillan, Harper-Collins, Hachette and Simon & Schuster) or are setting out on your own as an indie author, editing is essential. You don't need to spend thousands of dollars to get your manuscript ready for sale. There are plenty of editors who offer their services for a low price. Some are college students looking for some extra income, or indie editors who are looking to set up a new career for themselves. Editors can offer to proofread to make sure your story flows and is not missing any key plot points, as well as correct grammar and spelling mistakes. Some also will offer formatting services.

I cannot stress enough how important it is to have your work edited. I know as an indie, it is hard to find extra cash for a book you probably think no one will read. Even if only one person picks up your work, you want it to be the best it can possibly be. Constant typos and punctuation mistakes can make the story difficult to follow and can lead to negative reviews.

I am a big fan of Grammarly[1] to help me self-edit while I write. It will cut down on your mistakes and make the manuscript easier to revise after going through an actual editor. Not only does it work within Microsoft Word but it also will help correct your spelling and punctuation on websites like Facebook.

---

1. https://app.grammarly.com/

There are also professional services that are affordable for independent authors. Many don't know that Kirkus not only offers professional reviews, but they also offer an editing service.[2]

What makes them stand out above the rest is that they only use editors who've worked with the BIG 5 publishers and understand exactly what is needed to make your novel stand out among the bestsellers. They also offer a tracking system so you can monitor the progress through the editorial process.

It's important to trust those you chose to work with and that's why I recommend using a professional service like the one Kirkus provides.

However, if you aren't ready to commit, a simple Google or Facebook search can put you in contact with thousands of editors. Adept Edits[3], Theresa Wegand Proofreading and Editing[4], Big Bang Book Services[5], Juli's Elite Editing[6] are just a few providers that come up with a Facebook search.

An excellent way to manage edits is to use track changes[7] in your Word document. It makes it easy for an editor to suggest changes and leave notes in the margin. If you are unsure of how to use track changes, click the link above for a tutorial.

---

2. https://www.kirkusreviews.com/editing-services/

3. https://www.facebook.com/adept.edits?fref=ts

4. https://www.facebook.com/pages/Theresa-Wegand-Proofreading-Editing/
   372002539538687

5. https://www.facebook.com/BigBangBookServices

6. https://www.facebook.com/JulisEliteEditing

7. http://www.youtube.com/watch?v=AUf-IxzXyVk

FORMATTING

FORMATTING IS WHAT makes your story look beautiful on mobile reading devices. It can be unpleasant to see a story where chapters begin in the middle of a page, or the font is too large. A lot of authors format their own novels, but I prefer to use a service so I can focus on the next step in the writing process. Remember, different sites require different formatting, such as Amazon and Barnes & Noble. I use Draft2Digital[1] for my indie releases. It's as simple as uploading your document and choosing the look that best suits your genre.

Amazon has instructions[2] on how their ebook should be formatted for their site. There are many different formats[3] for ebooks and which you use depends on the site it will be uploaded to. It can be overwhelming for someone with little computer knowledge, but luckily, there are many people who will provide this service for you at low cost.

It is imperative that you take the time to have your novel professionally edited and formatted. I cannot stress this enough. You may have written the best book on the planet, but if it is hard to read, you will not find a fan base and your work will not be taken seriously. It is hard enough to compete with the millions of books on the market today, make sure you give yourself a fighting chance.

1. https://www.draft2digital.com/

2. https://kdp.amazon.com/self-publishing/help?topicId=A17W8UM0MMSQX6

3. http://en.wikipedia.org/wiki/Comparison_of_e-book_formats

Make sure you add acknowledgments and also information on what other novels you have published or will be publishing in the future. You can even add a snippet in the back.

Don't forget to use a copyright at the beginning of the book.

You can use the example below:

Author Name

Title book

© 2012, Author

Publisher

(Possibly email address or contact data)

ALL RIGHTS RESERVED. This book contains material protected under International and Federal Copyright Laws and Treaties. Any unauthorized reprint or use of this material is prohibited. No part of this book may be reproduced or transmitted in any form or by any means, electronic or mechanical, including photocopying, recording, or by any information storage and retrieval system without express written permission from the author/publisher.

COVER DESIGN

THEY SAY TO NEVER JUDGE a book by its cover, but we all do. Packaging is essential to getting someone to notice your work. Flipping through page after page of ebooks on sites such as Amazon or Barnes & Noble, you want a reader to take a second look at your book. You can do that by having a catchy title and cover.

The title should be something relevant to the story but leaves a little mystery. It should be short and easy to pronounce. Whenever I chose a new title, I do a quick search on Amazon to make sure it hasn't been used or at least not in my genre. If your title is too vulgar, it may turn readers off, even if they are looking for a steamy romance. Keep it simple and remember they may be reading the paperback in public.

Once you have picked a title, it is time to make a cover. As an indie author, cover designers may be out of your budget. That's okay. I make 99% of my own covers and I don't even use expensive programs such as Photoshop. If you are familiar with that program, it is an excellent tool for making covers and teasers, but I like to keep it simple.

If cover designers are out of your budget, you don't need to seek out a model and hire a photographer for a photo shoot. You can find lots of great images online. One of my favorite sites to find cover photos is DepositPhotos[1]. You can buy high quality images

---

1. https://depositphotos.com/

on a budget. The images come in different sizes and license options, depending on what you need. They run sales throughout the year and you can score a deal that would give you one-hundred photos for only one-hundred dollars.

I highly suggest running the image through a google image search to make sure it has not been used on other ebooks. To do this, just go to Google Images[2]. In the search bar, you will see an icon for a camera. Click on that and it will give you the option to upload an image to search. If you have found an image that you simply love and want to make sure it is not used in the future, you can contact the site or the photographer and offer to buy exclusive rights to that image. Understand that this does not affect those who purchased the image beforehand and it can also be very pricey. Most image rights can sell for upwards of seven hundred dollars. If you do happen to know a photographer or a model, this may be the best option for you to have a unique cover with little cost. Some models and photographers only asked to be listed in the acknowledgments.

Another great stock photo site[3] is Shutterstock[4]. Their photos are inexpensive and you can purchase yearly subscriptions or a set number of downloads. It is entirely up to you.

Once you have your image and title, you need to make your cover. Like I've mentioned before, I do not know how to use Pho-

---

2. http://www.google.com/imghp

3. https://www.google.com/#q_43ec3e5dee6e706af7766ff-
   fea512721_stock_26b17225b626fb9238849fd60eabdf60_pho-
   to_26b17225b626fb9238849fd60eabdf60_sites

4. http://www.shutterstock.com/

toShop. Instead, I use a combination of PaintShop (yes, the one that comes with your laptop) and PicMonkey[5]. This site is free, with a paid option to give you more font choices. You can upload an image and add fonts, move them around, change effects and all for free. It is great for beginners because it is extremely user-friendly.

You want to make sure that whatever image you chose, it looks good as a thumbnail on purchase sites. Often, the reader only gets a glimpse of a small image and if they are unable to make out what the picture is, they may never click on your book.

To create a full jacket i.e. paperback cover, you can create this using a Createspace template when you upload your novel or you can download a template and create one yourself. I find it easier to use their site so I don't have to guess about the width of the spine. If you would like to download their template[6], you just need to know how many pages your paperback will be. You know this from uploading your novel (which I explain later in the guide) and the size of the book. Remember, different sites require different image sizes. Barnes & Noble requires a smaller image than Amazon. For this, I just open my cover in PaintShop and resize it to fifty percent.

---

5. http://picmonkey.com/

6. https://www.createspace.com/Help/Book/Artwork.do

SYNOPSIS

———

YOU HAVE MADE YOUR cover and catchy title to get a reader to click on your book. Now you need to make them want to read it. This is where the synopsis comes in. You want to describe your novel in a short paragraph, without giving away the entire plot. The reader needs to be left wanting more. It can be difficult to sum up a story that took you one hundred thousand words to say in just a few short sentences. I recommend asking your beta reader to look over your synopsis. They know what your story is about and will find out if you have given too much away, or may have missed out on something they found to be important.

Make sure to leave the reader wanting more. They need to know what the hero's secret is or why he has vowed to never fall in love again. You can also use a simple line from the synopsis as a tagline on the front cover. Some examples of a tagline are: *There are two sides to every story* (for a duel point of view novel) or *Our love is worth dying for* (used for a vampire romance).

PROMOTION

———

PROMOTING YOUR STORY incredibly important. With millions of books on the market, how else will anyone know you have a book coming out if you don't tell them?

I like to make teasers and they are incredibly easy to throw together. I use Picmonkey (the service we talked about in the last chapter). I purchase a few pictures from a stock photo site and add in a snippet from my story. You don't want to give anything away, so make sure your teaser leaves a reader wanting to know more. You can also post snippets that are a few paragraphs long to help gain interest. Always be sure to include a buy link if your novel is already on the market or preorder links.

Another great way to gain interest is to make a book trailer. These are kind of like movie trailers. You can purchase videos and pictures from stock sites, to avoid copyright infringement. Add a song that will get the reader in the mood and a few captions to help them understand what the story is about. I use Windows Movie Maker. It is a program that came with my laptop, but there are also services out there that you can purchase to have a trailer made. CorrCommercials[1] offers professional trailers for a competitive price.

Cards, pens, and posters are great for giveaways. You can custom order through sites such as VistaPrint[2]. They are also great for gifts at book signings. I have ordered postcards and used the

---

1. https://corrcommercials.com/

front as the cover and the back as the synopsis (back cover of the book). They are great to sign and inexpensive to mail out to winners.

Paying for ads on Facebook or promoting posts helps to get your work seen by a larger crowd. You can also pay for an ad on sites like Goodreads.

I make Spotify playlists for every book I write. I have found that readers love to listen to the music that inspired the characters. They can subscribe to your playlists and listen along while they read. That's just another way to let the reader inside of your head.

Giveaways are an excellent way to get readers involved. The easiest way to set up a giveaway is through Rafflecopter[3]. You can completely customize it to what suits you best. I suggest making a few mandatory options to enter such as share the giveaway on Facebook and Twitter. This will help spread the word for you. If gift cards and Kindles are out of your price range, give away copies of your ebooks.

It is always important to give your books to bloggers. They reach a large reader base and will be able to help get your name out there. I will talk about bloggers and blog tours in a later chapter.

I do not personally use a street team to advertise but have known many authors who have and love them. It can be a group of readers or even friends and family that help share teasers and spread

---

2. http://www.vistaprint.com/vp/ns/default.as-

   px?mk=Vista&ad=e&query=vista&crtv=3364363725&psite=mkwid%7ckg-

   PR097X&GP=10%2f30%2f2013+1%3a38%3a47+PM&GPS=2994316353&GNF=0

3. http://www.rafflecopter.com/

the word about upcoming releases and giveaways. You can set up your own private group on Facebook to help relay information and make your job just a little bit easier.

Bloggers are crucial to getting your new release out to the readers. If you do not know any bloggers personally, post a message on your like page asking if any bloggers would like to have an ARC (Advanced Readers Copy) to review for your release.

You can also set up a blog tour. This is usually hosted by a blog that will find others who like to read your genre. They will set dates for others to post reviews, teasers, and snippets. It is also a good idea to include a giveaway that ends on your release day, or shortly after. It is important to get your manuscript and other valuable material to them promptly because they are, after all, doing you a favor.

If you don't want to have a tour, you can reach out to bloggers to do a review. Almost every blog has a contact option on their site with specific information that they require from you. Every blogger is different and most get many requests, so make sure you follow their instructions.

I keep a list of bloggers who I have worked with in the past so I can quickly send out ARCs of my next novel. Google Docs[4] is an excellent way to relay information for a tour that everyone can access.

---

4. https://accounts.google.com/ServiceLogin?service=writely&passive=1209600&contin-

ue=https%3A%2F%2Fdocs.google.com%2F%3Furp%3Dhttps%3A%2F%2Fwww.google

lowup=https%3A%2F%2Fdocs.google.com%2F%3Furp%3Dhttps%3A%2F%2Fwww.go

pl=homepage

MARKETING YOURSELF

———

IT IS VITALLY IMPORTANT to be available to our readers. Create a Facebook LIKE page[1]. It is an excellent way to give information about future releases. Most authors prefer to keep their profile private, so they have a place to chat with friends and family and their LIKE page is specifically for readers. I use both. Set up a Twitter profile[2] and connect it to your LIKE page so your posts automatically are displayed in both places. This will save you time and the headache of having to repost your information on every site. Post an update at least once a week, but remember, this is to keep in touch with readers so keep it professional.

Other social networks such as Google+[3] are also an excellent way to stay in touch with your fan base. Goodreads[4] lets you set up an author profile where you can list your books for readers to leave reviews. I highly recommend that if you use a site with reviews, not to comment or even read them. It will only stifle your creativity for the future. Shelfari[5] is another site that lists your books and it is connected to Amazon, so if you post information about your characters, it will feed through to your buy page on

---

1. https://www.facebook.com/pages/create/?ref_id=254913527873027

2. https://twitter.com/

3. https://accounts.google.com/ServiceLogin?service=oz&passive=1209600&continue=https://plus.google.com/?gpsrc%3Dgplp0%26partnerid%3Dgplp0

4. http://www.goodreads.com/

5. http://www.shelfari.com/

Amazon.com. This is an excellent way to give readers more details about your books before purchasing.

Amazon Author Central[6] is a great tool to edit your book information and check out your rankings. Be sure to fill out your profile on all of the different Amazon sites for different countries. The information does not carry over for each one. Fill out your profile information on Amazon.com[7], Amazon.co.uk[8], Amazon.de[9] , Amazon.fr[10] , Amazon.co.jp[11]. These links go directly to Author Central on each site. The other Amazon sites have yet to set up an Author Central, but they should come in the near future. Readers browsing books love to check out an author and see who they are and how to contact them. You can upload book trailers as well as link your blog and Twitter feed.

Having an official website is a great way for readers to find more of your work. You can hire someone to design it and give you all the bells and whistles, but you can also create a user-friendly space all by yourself. I use Weebly[12]. You can set up a site for free using their extension ex: SampleName.weebly.com or you can pay a small fee per year to have your own domain name ex: SampleName.com. It is very user-friendly and includes a blog so you can keep your readers up to date with any news you want to share. If you aren't up for creating a website, I highly recommend

6. https://authorcentral.amazon.com/gp/home

7. https://authorcentral.amazon.com/#sthash.qL3NDIRY.dpuf

8. https://authorcentral.amazon.co.uk/#sthash.qL3NDIRY.dpuf

9. https://authorcentral.amazon.de/#sthash.qL3NDIRY.dpuf

10. https://authorcentral.amazon.fr/

11. https://authorcentral.amazon.co.jp/

12. http://www.weebly.com/

having a blog. There are many free sites that offer blog hosting such as Wordpress[13] and Blogster[14]. If typing out a blog doesn't interest you, start a Youtube[15] channel (which you should already have for book trailers) and upload a short video update there.

Make sure you have an e-mail address for fans. This is a great way for them to get in touch with you if they would like to review your book, an agent is interested in representing you, or if a publisher would like to chat. Yahoo and Gmail are free and easy to set up. Also, if you want readers to be able to send you books to sign, it may be a good idea to set up a P.O. box so you aren't giving out your home address. You can do this at your local post office and it only costs a few bucks per year.

---

13. http://wordpress.com/

14. http://www.blogster.com/

15. http://youtube.com/

SELLING YOUR NOVEL

YOU'VE POURED BLOOD, sweat, and tears into your work of art and now it is finally time to share it with the world. The best day to publish is usually a Tuesday. This gives you a full week of sales and a better chance to make the bestseller lists and also makes sure that if your pre-order profits are released early, they still count in that initial week. If you aren't concerned with the lists just yet, a Friday release may be right to get the weekend readers. Announce your release date several weeks before you are actually ready to hit publish. Also, make sure to set up a Blog Tour and post lots of teasers to get a reader excited.

There are new ebook retailers popping up daily, but I will list a few of the important ones. Amazon is by far the largest ebook retailer in the business. First, you sign up for their author program[1]. It is quick and painless. Next, you upload your formatted and edited manuscript with all of the details. You can choose your selling price and even opt for the KDP Select program[2]. This will give new authors the opportunity to give their ebook away for free on their site and be a part of the Kindle Lending Library. You can earn money based off of how many times your book has been borrowed from their program. The only drawback is that you must sell exclusively through them for a certain amount of time. They are the largest ebook retailer, and where most indie authors will make the bulk of their profit. But by sell-

---

1. https://kdp.amazon.com/self-publishing/signin

2. https://kdp.amazon.com/self-publishing/KDPSelect

ing only through one retailer, you won't be eligible to make any of the bestseller lists, such as New York Times or USA Today. While that may seem like a far-off dream, many indie authors do make these lists and it is important to keep your options open. Remember, it can take several days for a novel to go live on Amazon so I suggest uploading, at least, two days before release date.

If you decide to set up a pre-order on Amazon, Smashwords, or Draft2Digital, you manuscript will need to be uploaded at least ten days before your official release date. Failure to do so can result in pre-order privileges being taken away and the loss of those sales you would have earned.

Pricing is a difficult decision to make. Most indie author's price low to get their book into more hands. Pricing your novel at ninety-nine cents will get you a lot of downloads, but those books bought at a discount are not necessarily read right away by the purchaser. Many people will buy books on sale to stock up for the future. I generally priced a novel that is over sixty thousand words at 2.99 when I first started out. I tend not to go more than that until you have gotten yourself established and have a fan base. Even after developing your own following, I would keep it around 3.99 – 4.99.

If you have decided to not go with selling exclusively through Amazon, you will need to upload to all of the other major sites. Luckily, sites like Smashwords[3] offer a premium library[4] that will upload to other major sites for you. You can even get a free ISBN[5]number[6] for your ebook through them. This is different

---

3. http://www.smashwords.com/

4. https://www.smashwords.com/distribution

from your ISBN used for paperbacks, which you can also get for free through Createspace.

Draft2Digital[7] is a one-stop shop for uploading to all major sites as well, including Amazon. The manuscript must pass upload requirements for all locations included for it to publish. Every site has different guidelines and you need to make sure you are following each one's rules to fast track your upload. I find Draft2Digital the easiest option.

Barnes & Noble has an indie program called NookPress[8] which allows you to upload your novel for sale. You can even use their site to write your story directly into their system, enabling you to edit and change just as you would with Word. Again, remember that upload times vary with each site and you should allow several days as a buffer before your release date.

Another major site is Apple's iBooks. If you own a Mac laptop you can upload directly to their site. Otherwise you will need to use Smashwords or Draft2Digital.

Kobo's indie upload site is called Writing Life[9] and allows indie pre-orders. It is very user-friendly with a step-by-step guide to upload.

---

5. https://www.smashwords.com/dashboard/ISBNManager

6. https://www.smashwords.com/dashboard/ISBNManager

7. https://draft2digital.com/

8. https://www.nookpress.com/projects

9. http://www.kobo.com/writinglife

Don't forget about your paperback! Createspace[10] is the easiest place that I have found for this but you can also use Draft2Digital or directly on Amazon's KDP site. You can upload your file, create your cover (if you haven't already) and you're good to go! Paperbacks take a few days to be checked for errors and after it has been approved, you can order a proof (that is just a fancy word for a copy of your book!). If you are confident that everything is perfect, you can bypass this option and approve it digitally, but I don't recommend doing this with your first novel. Paperbacks can take several days to populate on Amazon.com, so be sure to allow yourself a week or two to get everything in order.

Once your paperback and e-book have made it to Amazon, you can link the two[11]so they show on the same page. It makes it easier for a reader so they don't have to search the site twice. The linking option is found in your KDP site under the help section.

Want your novel to be available as an audiobook on Audible[12]? ACX[13] makes it easy for indie authors to have their books professionally narrated. You can choose the voice that perfectly fits your story and even pay with a share of the royalties (earnings) instead of having to pay upfront.

---

10. https://www.createspace.com/

11. https://kdp.amazon.com/self-publishing/help?topicId=A33G45HCUNE6YF

12. http://www.audible.com/

13. http://www.acx.com/

SALES & RANK

———

YOUR WORK DOESN'T END after you've hit published. You need to continue to promote your job and begin thinking about your next project. The key to being successful is good time management. One day you may be editing a manuscript and the next you will be writing. The day after you may be making a cover for a future project. There is always something to do.

Obsessing over sales, ranking and reviews can consume your time and it is important to stay focused. You've already done something most only dream of. You're an author. You don't need a check, a number or a five-star review to tell you that.

The first time I hit publish I barely sold anything. I stared at the screen just hoping one person would buy a copy. You can't judge your worth as a writer by the books you sell. It doesn't happen overnight. It can take years and years of hard work before you see any success. Some books don't find their fan base for years after release.

Obviously, if you aren't making sales, your rank is not going to jump. This doesn't mean the Joe Shmo, who is number one in the Kindle store, is a better writer than you. This just says Joe stuck through it when others would have given up. It can often seem like everyone around you is an overnight success, but that is because before that author was a household name, they spend every day perfecting their craft.

You may love to write paranormal books and right now everyone is clamoring for contemporary romance. That doesn't mean stop writing about what you love, that just means you will need to be patient. What's popular today may not be what's popular tomorrow.

I've heard a million times over, "Why is so and so a bestseller? Their books aren't any good!" What you love to read might be entirely different as what someone else likes to read. Don't bash others for finding success. Your time will come. That also brings me to my next point: Reviews.

REVIEWS

REVIEWS CAN KILL YOUR creativity. Not everyone will love your book. In fact, I can guarantee you that someone will hate it. It is a fact. Like death and taxes, you will get a bad review. Many people will tell you to ignore reviews. Never read them. To be honest, when I started writing I read every single review I received. Did it hurt? Absolutely. But I also learned. I learned how to become a better writer and give the readers what they wanted. That doesn't mean writing for someone else, I still write the story that I want to tell. If I want to kill off a character, that is what I do. But I have learned to give more dimension to secondary characters. I've learned the importance of fleshing out a scene.

Do I have thick skin? No. I don't. I still get my feelings hurt and I still complain to my friends that I don't think I'm good enough. I believe that it is important for a writer to be sensitive. But I also know that being upset will not help me reach my goals in life. I get over it. I no longer read reviews, not because I think I don't have more to learn, I do, but because it does stifle creativity. Not all negative reviews have constructive criticism. In fact, some are just down right mean. Who needs that? I don't and neither do you. Reviews are for other readers. They are not for the authors. Some of the most successful authors of all time have scathing reviews. It happens.

You can still learn and grow without reading the negative feedback and I recommend this as the way to go. You're not perfect and no matter how hard you try, you will never be, but you can always grow and learn. That's what life is about.

Pat yourself on the back for being awesome and get to work! Your next book isn't going to write itself!

Don't miss out!

Click the button below and you can sign up to receive emails whenever Teresa Mummert publishes a new book. There's no charge and no obligation.

https://books2read.com/r/B-A-BVD-QPMF

Connecting independent readers to independent writers.

Also by Teresa Mummert

Hollow Point Series
Hollow

Honor Series
Honor Student
Honor Thy Teacher
Honor and Obey
Honor and Betray

Shame On You
Shameless

Standalone
The Note
Safe Word
Bleed Ink: A Self-Publishing Guide

Perfect Lie
Pretty Little Things
Rellik
The Good Girls
Something Wicked
The Death of Lila Jane
Crave

Watch for more at www.TeresaMummert.com.

About the Author

TERESA MUMMERT grew up in a small town in Pennsylvania where she began dating her husband when they were only sixteen years old. They married at eighteen and soon moved to Louisiana as her husband began his military career. They are the proud parents of four children that they are raising in Georgia.

Teresa began writing when her husband was deployed to Afghanistan as a way to cope with him being away at war. She soon became a *New York Times* and *USA Today* bestselling author. Her work includes the word of mouth bestselling, *White Trash Trilogy*, which landed her a three book publishing deal with Simon & Schuster. That series includes *White Trash Beautiful*, *White Trash Damaged*, and *A Song For Us*. She has also written the *New York Times* and *USA Today* bestselling novel *The Note*, the *USA Today* bestselling novel *Safe Word*, as well as *Perfect Lie*, *Pretty Little Things*, *Honor Student*, *Honor Thy Teacher*, *Honor and Obey*, *Honor and Betray*, *Rellik*, *The Good Girls*, *Something Wicked*, *The Death of Lila Jane*, *Crave*, *Hollow*, the *USA Today* bestselling co- written novel *Sweet Nothing*, and her newest New Adult novel *Shameless*.

Find Teresa at TeresaMummert.com
Facebook: Facebook.com/TeresaMummert
Twitter: Twitter.com/TeresaMummert

Instagram: Instagram.com/TeresaMummert
Pinterest: Pinterest.com/TeresaMummert
Read more at www.TeresaMummert.com.